"*The Purity Principle* clearly presents the benefits of choosing purity and the consequences of choosing impurity. Randy Alcorn shows us how to get clean and stay clean!"

DENNIS RAINEY, PRESIDENT OF FAMILYLIFE

"This is a powerful little book! Randy Alcorn removes the glimmer of sexual impurity—and shows why purity is a million times better."

JOSHUA HARRIS, AUTHOR OF *BOY MEETS GIRL* AND *I KISSED DATING GOODBYE*

"*The Purity Principle* is a lifeline to help you stay the course in experiencing moral purity. Read it and pass it on to your spouse, children, and friends. They will be forever grateful!"

DR. GARY AND BARBARA ROSBERG, AUTHORS OF *DIVORCE-PROOF YOUR MARRIAGE*

"With a pastor's heart and a prophet's directness, Randy Alcorn issues a greatly needed warning about the choices that lead to moral failure. His biblical and practical counsel will instead lead to moral freedom, blessing, and great joy."

NANCY LEIGH DEMOSS, HOST OF *REVIVE OUR HEARTS*, AUTHOR OF *LIES WOMEN BELIEVE*

OTHER BOOKS BY RANDY ALCORN

FICTION

Deception
Deadline
Dominion
Edge of Eternity
Lord Foulgrin's Letters
Ishbane Conspiracy
Safely Home

NONFICTION

In Light of Eternity
Law of Rewards
Money, Possessions, and Eternity
ProLife Answers to ProChoice Arguments
Restoring Sexual Sanity
Sexual Temptation
The Grace and Truth Paradox
The Treasure Principle
Women Under Stress
Why Pro-Life?

The
PURITY
PRINCIPLE

LifeChange Books

RANDY
ALCORN

Multnomah Books

THE PURITY PRINCIPLE
published by Multnomah Books
A division of Random House, Inc.

© 2003 by Eternal Perspective Ministries
International Standard Book Number: 1-59052-195-1

Cover image by Bilderberg/Photonica

Unless otherwise indicated, Scripture quotations are from:
The Holy Bible, New International Version
© 1973, 1984 by International Bible Society,
used by permission of Zondervan Publishing House
Other Scripture quotations are from:
The New Testament in Modern English, Revised Edition (Phillips)
© 1958, 1960, 1972 by J. B. Phillips
New American Standard Bible® (NASB) © 1960, 1977, 1995
by the Lockman Foundation. Used by permission.
The Holy Bible, King James Version (KJV)

Multnomah is a trademark of Multnomah Publishers
and is registered in the U.S. Patent and Trademark Office.
The colophon is a trademark of Multnomah Publishers.

Printed in the United States of America

For information:
MULTNOMAH BOOKS
12265 ORACLE BOULEVARD, SUITE 200
COLORADO SPRINGS, CO 80921

Library of Congress Cataloging-in-Publication Data

Alcorn, Randy C.
   The purity principle / by Randy Alcorn.
       p. cm.
Includes bibliographical references.
   ISBN 1-59052-195-1
   1. Sex—Religious aspects—Christianity. 2. Chastity. 3. Sexual abstinence—Religious
aspects—Christianity.   I. Title.

   BT708.A435 2003
   241'.66—dc21

                                        2003005461

                        07 08—12 11 10 9

To my brothers and sisters who are now overcomers for Jesus, having turned away from lesser and fraudulent pleasures to joyfully embrace pleasures both greater and true.

"In thy presence is fulness of joy; at thy right hand there are pleasures for evermore."
PSALM 16:11, KJV

Contents

ACKNOWLEDGMENTS

I want to recognize the vital assistance of my editor and friend, Larry Libby, who took what I'd written and helped select and distill it to fit on these pages. Larry also came up with the Jonah 2:8 application, which I'd never thought of before in relation to sexual purity. Special thanks also to SL, NR, HT, and NK for their valuable input on the manuscript.

Chapter 1

FORFEITING WHAT
COULD HAVE BEEN

Eric stormed into my office and flopped into a chair. "I'm really mad at God."

Having grown up in a strong church family, he'd met and married a Christian girl. Now he was the picture of misery.

"Okay…so why are you mad at God?"

"Because," he said, "last week I committed adultery."

Long pause. Finally I said, "I can see why God would be mad at you. But why are *you* mad at *God?*"

Eric explained that for several months he'd felt a strong, mutual attraction with a woman at his office. He'd prayed earnestly that God would keep him from immorality.

"Did you ask your wife to pray for you?" I said. "Did

you stay away from the woman?"

"Well...no. We went out for lunch almost every day."

Slowly I started pushing a big book across my desk. Eric watched, uncomprehending, as the book inched closer and closer to the edge. I prayed aloud, "O Lord, please keep this book from falling!"

I kept pushing and praying. God didn't suspend the law of gravity. The book went right over the edge, smacking the floor.

"I'm mad at God," I said to Eric. "I asked Him to keep my book from falling...but He let me down!"

The Choices That Ruin Us

To this day, I can still hear the sound of that book hitting the floor. It was a picture of Eric's life. Young, gifted, and blessed with a wife and little girl, Eric brimmed with potential.

His story didn't end that day. Eventually he became a sexual predator, molesting his own daughter. He's been in prison for years now, repentant but suffering the consequences of inching his life toward the edge until gravity took over.

How many of us Christians hope God will guard us from calamity and misery, while every day we make small, seemingly inconsequential immoral choices that inch us toward bigger immoralities? (A survey taken at a Promise Keepers gathering of 1,500 Christian men revealed that half of them had viewed pornography the previous week.)

Tiffany and Kyle also grew up in the church. When the youth pastor warned against premarital sex, they had trouble taking him seriously. Their movies, television, and music focused on sex. One night after youth group, Tiffany gave in to Kyle. It was painful, nauseating...nothing like in the movies. Afterward she felt horrible. Kyle was mad at her because she wasn't supposed to let it happen.

Tiffany started sleeping around, trying to find a guy who'd love her. She never did—they just used her and moved on. She quit going to church. One day she discovered she was pregnant. A friend drove her to an abortion clinic. Now she's plagued by dreams about the child she killed.

Tiffany could turn to Christ. He would forgive her. But her heart is so broken and calloused now, she doesn't believe it. She's attempted suicide. She's on drugs, a street prostitute. She's been raped. Recently she had another abortion. Her eyes are dead. So is her hope.

Kyle? He's lost interest in spiritual things. He's at college now, an atheist. He's had sex with several girls. He feels empty but experiments with anything he thinks might bring him happiness.

Lucinda, a Christian, decided her husband wasn't romantic enough. A decent, hardworking, church-going guy, he just didn't live up to the Prince Charming images of

Hollywood. She got involved with another man, eventually marrying him. Years later, after bringing unspeakable grief to her family and herself, she came back to Christ. "I wish I had my first husband back," she admitted. "But now it's too late." Yes, God has forgiven Lucinda and still has plans for her. And yet…she has paid a fearful price.

The prophet Jonah, in the digestive tract of a great fish beneath the Mediterranean Sea, made this observation: "Those who cling to worthless idols forfeit the grace that could be theirs" (Jonah 2:8).

An idol is something more than a grotesque statue with big lips and a ruby in its navel. It's a God-substitute. It's something—anything—that we value higher than God. In order to cling to such an idol, we make a trade.

Our sexual behavior reveals who or what rules our lives (see Romans 1:18–29). Sexual sin is idolatry because it puts our desires in the place of God.

Those who turn from God to embrace a God-substitute suffer terrible loss. Why? Because they were made to find joy in God, not the substitute. They swap God's present and future blessing for something they can immediately see, taste, or feel. But that something *never* satisfies.

I've done it. So have you. To one degree or another, every sinner trades what they have—and could have had—for a lie. Sometimes the lies get bigger and the stakes get higher. We keep inching our lives toward destruction. To fulfill some hormonal surge, some secret fantasy, we willingly trade our future.

It's a terrible trade. A deal with the devil, who never keeps his bargains.

Every day, Christian men and women forfeit future happiness for the sake of temporary sexual stimulation. Like drug addicts, we go from fix to fix, trading the contentment of righteous living for the quick hits that always leave us empty, craving more.

That's what Eric did.

He forfeited a wife who loved him…a daughter who would have adored him…the respect of his family, friends, coworkers, and church. A walk with Christ.

In the end, he forfeited his freedom.

With every little glance that fuels our lust, we push ourselves closer to the edge, where gravity will take over and bring our lives crashing down.

What will we lose? What will we forfeit that could have, *would* have been ours?

Where would Tiffany be now if she'd kept herself pure? Instead of a prostitute haunted by rapes and abortions, Tiffany could be a light for Jesus, standing up for Him on a college campus, filled with joy and hope for the future. Kyle might be that too—*if only*.

What about Lucinda? She also forfeited what was hers—and could have been hers. Who knows what God's grace might have included. *A clear conscience and a priceless sense of peace? Warm, satisfying years of companionship? The respect and affection of children and grandchildren? An enduring influence on young women watching her example? A ministry touching scores of lives? Rewards—exceeding all imagination—in the life to come?*

Yes, God has forgiven her. Absolutely. But the consequences of her choices remain.

Some readers, choking on consequences, feel hopeless and defeated. Many have given up on purity. Others have never tried. We all need foresight to see where today's choices will leave us tomorrow.

Once lost, some opportunities are never regained. We can't live in the "might-have-beens"—except to admit their reality, and then, by God's grace, move on.

In C. S. Lewis's *Prince Caspian,* after disregarding his instructions to follow him, Lucy tried to ask Aslan what might have happened if she had obeyed his voice sooner, following him instead of making excuses. The Great Lion replied, "To know what *would* have happened, child?... No. Nobody is ever told that."

Chapter 2

ENLIGHTENED
SELF-INTEREST

Here's what's striking about Eric, Lucinda, Tiffany and Kyle. *They all thought they were acting in their own best interests when they followed their lusts.* If we could have obtained an honest interview with any of them just before they trashed their purity, they would have said, "This is for *me*. This is for *my* happiness."

Yet it wasn't.

Not even close.

It never is.

In fact, they didn't just hurt others. Without intending to, they acted against their own self-interests.

What they did wasn't just wrong. *It was stupid.*

Since the time we were young teenagers, many of us

have heard lists of reasons for walking in sexual purity. God commands purity and forbids impurity. Purity is right. Impurity is wrong.

True? Absolutely. But it's equally correct to say *purity is always smart; impurity is always stupid.*

There it is—what I'm calling The Purity Principle:

Purity is always smart; impurity is always stupid.

Not sometimes.

Not usually.

Always. You're not an exception. I'm not an exception. There are no exceptions.

A holy God made the universe in such a way that actions true to His character, and the laws derived from His character, are *always* rewarded. Actions that violate His character, however, are *always* punished. He rewards every act of justice; He punishes every act of injustice.

That doesn't mean God always intervenes directly. This moral law is like the law of gravity. God has set it in place. When a careless driver speeds on an icy mountain pass, loses control, and plunges his car off a cliff, God doesn't suddenly invent gravity to punish the driver's carelessness. Gravity is already in place.

In the same way, God doesn't need to punish the pornography addict for every wrong choice. *The punishment is built into the sin.* Shame, degradation, and warping of the personality follow as a matter of course. Scripture describes those who have surrendered to their lust to live in immorality as "receiving in their own persons the due penalty of their error" (Romans 1:27, NASB).

That's the way God's moral universe operates. We get to choose our own path. But with each path comes inevitable consequences.

The roads of life are sometimes hazardous. But God loves us enough to place warning signs: "Don't commit adultery" and "No sex before marriage." We don't have to obey. We do have to live with the consequences.

Purity is safe. Impurity is risky. Purity always helps us. Impurity always hurts us. *Purity is always smart; impurity is always stupid.* Write it down. Bank on it.

Consider Christ's story of two men:

> "Everyone who hears these words of mine and puts them into practice is like a wise man who built his house on the rock. The rain came down, the streams rose, and the winds blew and beat against that house; yet it did not fall, because it had its foundation on the rock. But everyone who hears these words of mine and does not put them into practice is like a foolish man who built his house on sand. The rain came down, the streams rose, and the winds blew and beat against that house, and it fell with a great crash."
>
> MATTHEW 7:24–27

Jesus measures obedience not by its virtue, but by its *wisdom.*

He measures disobedience not by its wrongness, but by its *foolishness.* The man doomed himself to a "great crash" by his own stupid decisions. The obedient man isn't called "righteous," but "wise."

He's just being smart.

Satan's greatest victories and our biggest defeats come when he gets us to ask, "Should I choose what God commands me...*or* should I do what's best for me?" The very framing of the question shows how badly we're deceived.

We will not consistently choose God's way until we come to understand that His way is *always* best for us.

MULTIPLE MOTIVATIONS

"But wait a minute," you may say. "You're talking about a selfish, unspiritual motivation here. Shouldn't a Christian's only motivation be loving God?"

No, apparently not.

Scripture provides us with multiple motivations for obeying God. Love is one. But the Bible clearly supplies us with two other motives that appeal directly to our self-interest: fear of God and hope of reward.

If we think these are unspiritual motives, then we're failing to grasp a central biblical doctrine.[1]

The fear of God is a profound respect for His holiness,

which includes a fear of the consequences of disobeying Him. Weighing these consequences can motivate us to purity.

We can also argue for purity because God is by nature a Rewarder (see Hebrews 11:6), and He will surely reward us for making choices that please Him. Obedience to His will and His way forms the underlying lattice for that rarest and most wonderful human condition—joy.

> "This day I call heaven and earth as witnesses against you that I have set before you life and death, blessings and curses. Now choose life, so that you and your children may live and that you may love the LORD your God, listen to his voice, and hold fast to him. For the LORD is your life."
>
> DEUTERONOMY 30:19–20

We can choose blessings: joy, peace, life, hope, and laughter. Or we can choose curses: misery, scars, a handful of ashes.

When Cain, humanity's firstborn, stood at a moral crossroads, God gently reasoned with him. "Why are you angry? And why has your countenance fallen? If you do well, will not your countenance be lifted up? And if you do not do well, sin is crouching at the door; and its desire is for you, but you must master it" (Genesis 4:6–7, NASB).

God was saying, "If you choose My plan, you'll find happiness. There will be a smile on your face. Sure, this is a fallen world. But if you say no to your sinful desires that want to master you, if you walk with Me, you'll experience My peace. If you reject My standards, you will be surrendered to forces that will tear your life apart."

The rest is history.

THE SMART AND STUPID ARGUMENT

Does God really argue for sexual purity on the basis that it's the smart choice, while impurity is stupid? Judge for yourself:

> Why be captivated, my son, by an adulteress? Why embrace the bosom of another man's wife? For a man's ways are in full view of the LORD, and he examines all his paths. The evil deeds of a wicked man ensnare him; the cords of his sin hold him fast. He will die for lack of discipline, led astray by his own great folly.
>
> PROVERBS 5:20–23

Why avoid adultery? Because God will see it and He will bring judgment. But even before judgment day "the cords of his sin hold him fast." The adulterer will be ensnared; he will die. He's the primary victim of his foolishness. In contrast, the man who remains pure can "rejoice" and "be captivated" by his wife's love, enjoying their sexual union (Proverbs 5:18–19).

In the next chapter God asks,

Can a man scoop fire into his lap
    without his clothes being burned?
Can a man walk on hot coals
    without his feet being scorched?
So is he who sleeps with another man's wife;
    no one who touches her will go unpunished.

Proverbs 6:27–29

Proverbs also depicts the man who is seduced into adultery as "an ox going to the slaughter" and like a deer or bird being killed by a hunter (Proverbs 7:21–27).

A believer recovering from sexual addiction told me, "Addicts always think they can get away with it. You won't change until you realize you can't."

I can *never* get away with sexual immorality. God wants me to remember that…for *my* sake.

Make Your Choice

One night as a young pastor I chose to view pornography. I felt terrible. I'd failed my Lord, my wife, my church. I'd been a fool. I caught a horrifying glimpse of what I could easily become. But shame did nothing to deliver me. I had to start thinking—and choosing—differently.

Do you really *want* to be like an ox led to slaughter? If so, then keep flirting with that man next door or the new receptionist at the office. Keep thinking about messing with that girl or boy who sits next to you in class. Keep watching those television commercials and sitcoms and movies that shoot sex at you like arrows. The slaughterhouse is exactly where you're headed.

But if you want something better, something wonderful, choose purity instead.

It's okay to be out there "for yourself" on this issue. It's *right* to guard your virginity! It's *good* for you to encourage your children to save themselves for marriage, not only for God's glory but *for their own happiness!*

It's completely fitting to hold out the prospect of grief and self-destruction as reasons to avoid impurity. That's exactly what Proverbs does.

One of our church's elders admitted to me, "There have been times when I've had serious temptations toward adultery. I'd like to say that my love for God and for my wife were enough to keep me from falling. But it came down to *sheer terror.* I was certain that if I traveled that road, God would let my life turn miserable."

He's a wise man. A man who acted in his own best interests. He knows impurity will be punished and purity will be rewarded, with heaven's payoffs. It would be a *lousy* trade. He was too smart to make it.

Is that a lesser, unworthy motivation? No! This brother never fell. He never shipwrecked his family. He never shamed his church. He never broke his wife's heart. He never devastated his children. He never trashed his ministry.

Do you think his wife and children are grateful for the fear of God that kept him pure in the face of dark temptations? Absolutely.

The fear of God shouldn't scare us out of our wits; it should scare us *into* them. "The fear of the LORD is a fountain of life, turning a man from the snares of death" (Proverbs 14:27).

Those who've succumbed to sexual temptation *did not* do so in their self-interest. Rather, they pursued what they *imagined* was their self-interest, what Satan deceived them into *thinking* was their self-interest. Had they pursued their *true* self-interest they would have run from temptation as from a slithering cobra or a live grenade. They would have embraced purity as a drowning person grabs a life preserver. And how different their lives and families would be today if they had!

When God calls on you to pursue purity, you are not being asked to do what will deprive you of joy. In fact, you are being called on to do what will bring you the greatest joy!

To choose purity is to put yourself under God's blessing. To choose impurity is to put yourself under God's curse.

It's your decision. You cast your vote with every choice. Those choices amount to one of two prayers:

- "God, bless me for obeying You."
- "God, curse me for disobeying You."

What's *your* voting record? Which prayer is being uttered by your choices today?

THE MOST STRATEGIC BATTLE

Surveys indicate that the sexual morality of today's Christians has become almost indistinguishable from that of non-Christians. It's often impossible to discern where the world ends and the church begins.

Our failure to follow the teachings of Scripture in this area undermines our ability to accomplish what God has called us to. Why? Because if we are just like the world, we have nothing to offer it. An unholy world will never be won to Christ by an unholy church.

Why is sexual purity such an integral part of a rewarding life? *Why* is premarital and extramarital sex so toxic to joy? Why have so many tried and tried and tried…yet failed and failed and failed? How can we avoid the lures and snares that lock us into bondage and tear away the abundant life?

It's no overstatement to call this a life-and-death issue. The hour it will take you to read the rest of this book could save you from disaster. It could set you on a course for which you—and your family—will always be grateful.

Chapter 3

WHAT'S THE BIG
DEAL ABOUT SEX?

Have you heard the old saying, "All sin is alike to God"?

Not according to Paul. He said to those in sex-saturated Corinth:

> Flee from sexual immorality. All other sins a man
> commits are outside his body, but he who sins sexually sins against his own body.
>
> 1 CORINTHIANS 6:18

Right from the get-go, there is something qualitatively different about sexual sin. Why? Because sex is not just something you do; sex is *someone you are.* When you have sex, you put your life on the line. You give away something you may never get back.

Purity and impurity are more than external issues of behavior, culture, and practice. They cut to the soul. They slice to the living core of who you are and who you will become.

Sex wasn't invented by Hollywood, Madonna, or some pervert in an Internet chat room. Sex was created by an infinitely holy God, wreathed in blinding light and glory, surrounded by radiant, holy angels. The goodness of sex stands or falls with the goodness of its Creator.

"God saw all that he had made, and it was very good" (Genesis 1:31). Sex was part of the "all" that was so good. Even after the fall, God's Word speaks openly of the pleasure of sex within marriage (see Proverbs 5:18–19; Song of Solomon 4:5; 7:1, 6–9).

Sex is the means by which children are conceived and marital intimacy is expressed. Both are very important to God. When sexual union takes place in its proper context, in a spirit of giving, the Creator smiles.

THE POWER OF SEX

Here's what makes The Purity Principle so important:

Sex is incredibly powerful; it's able to do immense good…or immense harm.

Fire is a gift of God. What would we do without it? Have you ever stared into a campfire on a cold, clear night, deep in the heart of a star-strewn wilderness? Yet when those same magical flames move outside their boundaries, what happens? Horrible devastation. Pain. Death.

The most magnificent gifts of God, taken outside their God-intended boundaries, become utterly ruinous. So it is with sex. Its potential for great good has a flip side—potential for great evil.

As long as a fire is contained in the fireplace, it keeps you warm. But if the fire is "set free," the house burns down.

I've walked through the smoldering ruins of people's lives devastated by immorality. I have shared their despair as they wonder if they can ever rebuild. (They can—but *believing* they can is another matter.) I cannot forget such scenes permanently imprinted in my soul.

In contrast, to embrace purity is to lay claim to a magnificent gift. Purity is incomparably beautiful...like the fragrance of a rose after a summer shower. And it's a beauty that will never end, because all who live in heaven will be pure (see Revelation 21:27).

WHERE ARE THE BOUNDARIES?

According to the Bible, the boundaries of sex are the boundaries of marriage. Sex and marriage go together. *Sexual union is intended as an expression of a lifelong commitment.* Apart from marriage, the lasting commitment is absent. So the sex act becomes a lie.

Sex is a privilege inseparable from the responsibilities of the sacred marriage covenant. To claim the privilege apart from the responsibility perverts God's intention. Every act of sex outside of marriage cheapens both.

Sex is designed to be the joining of two persons, of two spirits, not just two bodies. Sex should be given to someone to whom you're 100 percent committed (as measured by legal marriage), not taken from someone to whom you're uncommitted.

"But we really love each other" has no bearing on the ethics of sexual intimacy. Sex does not become permissible through subjective feelings, but only through the objective, lifelong commitment of marriage. Those are God's rules. There's nothing we can do to change them. The rules are always enforced. When we break them, they always break us.

A smart traveler doesn't curse guardrails. He doesn't whine, "That guardrail dented my fender!" He looks over the cliff, sees demolished autos, and *thanks God* for guardrails.

God's guardrails are His moral laws. They stand between us and destruction. They are there not to punish or deprive us, but to protect us.

PURITY AND GOD'S WILL

Paul writes a highly charged paragraph on sexual purity, resounding with the "smart vs. stupid" theme:

It is God's will that you should be sanctified: that you should avoid sexual immorality; that each of you should learn to control his own body in a way that is holy and honorable, not in passionate lust like the heathen, who do not know God.... The Lord will punish men for all such sins, as we have already told you and warned you. For God did not call us to be impure, but to live a holy life. Therefore, he who rejects this instruction does not reject man but God, who gives you his Holy Spirit.

1 THESSALONIANS 4:3–8

How many times have you heard people talk about "finding God's will"? We speak of God's will as if it were lost or as though it were some Rubik's Cube that takes long years and the brains of Einstein to unravel.

But you don't have to wonder where God stands on sex outside of marriage. *"It is God's will that you should be sanctified [set apart, or holy]; that you should avoid sexual immorality."*

How clear is that?

Many people are "searching for God's will"—but many of those same people don't bother to live by what Scripture *says* is God's will. What's the point of seeking God's will in less important things if you're ignoring what He has *already told you:* to be pure?

Christ's disciples did not live by lust, which truly set them apart from the pagan culture around them. The church today needs to rediscover that critical aspect of our identity, as His spotless bride.

The problem isn't *passion,* but lust. We serve a *passionate* God. We should love and serve Him *passionately.* But we need to cultivate our passions for the right object, not the wrong ones.

"Learn to control his own body" means it doesn't come naturally—otherwise you wouldn't have to learn it. It requires training and discipline.

Resisting temptation is a gutsy, courageous, stubborn refusal to violate God's law. It's repeatedly calling upon Christ for the strength to say no to the world, the flesh, and the devil—to say yes to God instead. We do this in pursuit of the ultimate joy that can be found only in knowing God.

Remember that Beatles song where Ringo Starr sang, "All I gotta do is act naturally"?

The truth is, if you act naturally you're toast.

But if you act *supernaturally,* drawing on the power of the indwelling Christ, you'll enjoy great personal benefits, now and later.

Do you want God's will? Truly? Then embrace purity. Learn to control your body. Refuse to take sexual advantage of anyone. In so doing you will avoid God's punishment and taste the joy of a life pleasing to Jesus.

WHO OWNS YOUR BODY?

Sometimes, when I'm speaking about purity, I ask to borrow a pencil. I then break it in half, throw it down, and stomp on it. Eyes widen across the room, accompanied by an audible gasp. I ask the audience why they're shocked. Someone always says, "Because you broke their pencil."

Then I explain that it really was *my* pencil, that I gave it to the person in advance and asked her to hand it back when I called on her. Suddenly, everything changes. Since it belongs to me, I have the right to do with it as I please. If it belongs to someone else, I have no such right.

So who does my body belong to?

> You are not your own; you were bought at a price.
> Therefore honor God with your body.
> 1 CORINTHIANS 6:19–20

When I came to Christ, the title of my life was transferred from me to God. I was bought and paid for. At what price? The shed blood of God. We are His by creation, and again by redemption. He has every right to tell me what to do with my mind and body. *I have no right to do whatever I want with my body.*

Fortunately for me, God always acts not only for His glory, but for my best interests. So I can fully trust that whatever He forbids would have hurt me…and whatever He commands will only help me.

Chapter 4

TARGETED AND VULNERABLE

If you are a Christian, you are a targeted man, a marked woman. The forces of evil have taken out a contract on you. Satan's out to get you. If he can't take you to hell, he'll do his best to make your life a hell on earth.

I remember with embarrassment when I was a Bible college student. I heard of a prominent Christian leader who'd committed immorality. Adultery? *That* would be the day! I knew I could *never* betray the Lord and my wife that way. Not me.

By God's grace, I've never had sex with anyone but my wife. But this is largely due to the fact that I wised up. I came to grips with a frightening truth: It really *could* happen to me. And I'd been a *fool* to think otherwise.

If you assume you'll never be burglarized, you'll leave the windows open and cash lying on the dresser. If you think you'll never fall morally, you'll live carelessly, failing to take precautions.

"Pride goes before destruction, a haughty spirit before a fall" (Proverbs 16:18). God gives us a choice—humble ourselves or He will humble us (see 1 Peter 5:5–6).

Don't kid yourself that it can never happen to you—it can. *And if you don't think it can, it almost certainly will.*

As a pastor, I was counseling a woman when it suddenly struck me that she was interested in me. And here's what frightened me. I'd sensed this from the beginning…but I'd been flattered by her attention.

Since I wasn't (yet) emotionally involved with her, I was tempted to rationalize. Deep down, though, I heard an alarm bell. I knew I was walking in a field laced with land mines. God reminded me that every adultery I knew of had begun with something "harmless."

So I ran.

I made other arrangements. She could continue counseling…with someone else. My decision may have offended her. But it was a small price. God only knows—and I don't want to—what might have happened otherwise.

We tend to be most vulnerable when we're tired, isolated, lonely, discouraged, depressed, angry, or struggling in our relationships; especially with our mate. Don't think for a moment demons don't know this or will hesitate to pounce on us in those very times. "When the devil had finished all this tempting, he left Him until an opportune time" (Luke 4:13).

Paul's warnings deserve a prominent place on our dashboards, desks, Day-Timers, and PalmPilots: "So, if you think you are standing firm, be careful that you don't fall!" (1 Corinthians 10:12).

Here's a paraphrase: "If you think you don't need to take precautions…you can spell your name *S-t-u-p-i-d.*"

IT'LL ALL COME OUT

Violating God's moral standards is like violating the law of gravity—you can't get away from it:

> Don't be under any illusion: you cannot make a fool of God! A man's harvest in life will depend entirely on what he sows. If he sows for his own lower nature his harvest will be the decay and death of his own nature. But if he sows for the Spirit he will reap the harvest of everlasting life by that Spirit. Let us not grow tired of doing good, for, unless we throw in our hand, the ultimate harvest is assured.
>
> GALATIANS 6:7–9, PHILLIPS

Sooner or later, sexual sin will be exposed. "You may be sure that your sin will find you out" (Numbers 32:23). Solomon said, "The man of integrity walks securely, but he who takes crooked paths will be found out" (Proverbs 10:9).

Here's a thought that should give everyone pause. *There's no such thing as a private moment.*

Jesus warned His disciples: "There is nothing concealed that will not be disclosed, or hidden that will not be made known. What you have said in the dark will be heard in the daylight, and what you have whispered in the ear in the inner rooms will be proclaimed from the roofs" (Luke 12:2–3).

One of Satan's oldest tactics is to weave a phony web of secrecy, casting an illusion of privacy over our sinful choices. He tells us, "No one is watching. No one will know."

But he's lying. Someone *is* watching—the Audience of One. Someone already knows. And in time, many will know.

We never get away with anything.

THE CONSEQUENCES OF SEXUAL SIN

Antibiotics prevent or cure some venereal diseases. Contraceptives reduce the chances of pregnancy. *But there is no contraceptive for the conscience.*

Medical science may eliminate some consequences of my sin. It cannot remove my accountability to God.

God says, "If anyone turns a deaf ear to the law, even his prayers are detestable" (Proverbs 28:9). If we're not practicing purity, it nullifies our prayers and our ministry.

Sexual sin blocks fellowship with God. If we are in immorality's grip, there's only one prayer He wants to hear—the prayer of confession and repentance.

Achan's sin caused thirty-six Israelites to die, as well as his family (see Joshua 7:1–26). God is sovereign in each person's life, but clearly, *the private sins of one individual can bring terrible consequences on others.*

Cindy was twelve when her father, a church leader, committed adultery with a woman in the church and left his family. Deeply hurt, Cindy's godly mother remarried hastily, unwisely, to an unbeliever.

The scandal penetrated the community. Cindy had to live with looks of pity and scorn whenever she walked through town. But it gets worse. Cindy has been through a long series of bad relationships with men, including repeated sexual compromises. Though fully responsible for her own actions, she's also reaping what her father sowed (see Exodus 20:5).

Every wife whose husband has been trapped in pornography will testify that it had a deep impact on their intimacy.

A man active in ministry resigned because of homosexual activities. I asked, "What could have been said to you that might have prevented this?" After a moment's thought, he replied, "If someone could have helped me envision the tragedy it would bring to my ministry and the disgrace it would bring to Christ's name, I might never have done it."

IDENTIFYING SATAN'S LIES

Jesus said of Satan, "When he lies, he speaks his native language, for he is a liar and the father of lies" (John 8:44).

Satan is a smooth and convincing liar. Jesus tells truth that sets us free (see John 8:32).

Paul says "we are not unaware of [Satan's] schemes" (2 Corinthians 2:11). But too often today we are. We need to identify what Satan does to destroy us—so we can see it coming and resist.

"Be self-controlled and alert. Your enemy the devil prowls around like a roaring lion looking for someone to devour" (1 Peter 5:8).

Sometimes, when a sexually provocative image appears, as I close my eyes or turn my head I envision a barbed fishhook at the end of a line. If I hesitate even a moment—if I even think about nibbling—I imagine it will pierce my tongue and rip my flesh. I'll be caught and reeled in. *But the lure's beautiful.* How else would our enemy hook and destroy us? Temptations always look good—otherwise they wouldn't be temptations.

But our God is infinitely more powerful than Satan: "The one who is in you is greater than the one who is in the world" (1 John 4:4).

His divine power has given us everything we need
for life and godliness through our knowledge of
him who called us by his own glory and goodness.

Through these he has given us his very great and
precious promises, so that through them you may
participate in the divine nature and escape the cor-
ruption in the world caused by evil desires.

2 PETER 1:3–4

God warned the first humans that, if they ate the forbidden fruit: "You will surely die." Satan said: "You will *not*
surely die." Every time we're tempted toward sexual sin, we
must choose between two voices—God's or Satan's.

Which will you believe?

SUPERIOR SATISFACTION

A sexual image lures my mind toward lust. The world, the
flesh, and the devil barrage me with messages: I will feel like
a man; it will relieve my pain, disappointment, stress; I'll be
happier. "God's just trying to keep something good from
you," demons whisper.

God's Word shows the lie for what it is. It tells me that
real happiness can be found only in Christ.

I'm left with the choice—trust Satan or trust God.

I must choose between sexual fantasies and intimacy
with God. I cannot have both. When I see that God offers
me joys and pleasures that sexual fantasies don't, this is a
breakthrough. But that breakthrough will come only when
I pursue God, making Him the object of my quest—and

when I realize that fantasies are only a cheap God-substitute. Running to them is running from God.

When my thirst for joy is satisfied by Christ, sin becomes unattractive. I say no to the passing pleasures of immorality, not because I do not want pleasure, but because I want *true* pleasure, a greater and lasting pleasure that can be found only in Christ.

John Piper writes,

> The fire of lust's pleasures must be fought with the fire of God's pleasures. If we try to fight the fire of lust with prohibitions and threats alone—even the terrible warnings of Jesus—we will fail. We must fight it with a massive promise of superior happiness. We must swallow up the little flicker of lust's pleasure in the conflagration of holy satisfaction.[2]

Those who drink of immorality are never satisfied (see John 4:13). Those who drink of Jesus are fully satisfied (see John 6:35). I can either have my thirst quenched in Jesus, or I can plunge deeper into sin in search of what's not there.

The rest of your life will be largely determined by how you answer this question:

Who will you believe?

Chapter 5

THE BATTLE IS IN YOUR MIND

Brad was a seminary student preparing for ministry. One night he argued with his wife. Upset, he drove to Starbucks to think things through. Soon Brad was engrossed in conversation with a young woman. A few hours later he was in bed with her.

Brad came to me, ashamed. "How can I tell my wife? Will she ever forgive me? It was so sudden—there was no warning. It came out of the clear blue sky!"

Or did it?

Brad had worked nonstop to put himself through seminary. He'd come to subtly resent his wife, seeing her and the children as obstacles. He no longer dated her or communicated with her on a deep level.

He'd been looking at provocative magazines. He'd watched raunchy movies. All of this culminated in the horrible episode that "happened without warning."

The truth is, sexual sin *never* comes out of the blue. It is the predictable result of natural processes. Relationships are neglected and a mind gets exposed to impurity.

Tomorrow's character is made out of today's thoughts. Temptation may come suddenly, but sin doesn't. Neither does moral and spiritual fiber. Both result from a process over which we *do* have control.

We become what we think. We forge our sexual morality through an ongoing series of choices and actions, including tiny indulgences and minuscule compromises. The eye lingers here…the mind loiters there. Like a photographic plate forming an image, our mind accumulates what we expose it to, godly or ungodly.

The battle is in our minds.

WHERE LUST COMES FROM

Commonly, someone who falls is taken by surprise. They ask, "Where did *that* come from?" The Bible gives a clear answer: "For out of the heart come evil thoughts, murder, adultery, sexual immorality" (Matthew 15:19–20).

Jesus put it succinctly:

"You have heard that it was said, 'Do not commit adultery.' But I tell you that anyone who looks at

a woman lustfully has already committed adultery
with her in his heart."

MATTHEW 5:27–28

The Pharisees emphasized the external. Jesus raised the
moral bar, saying that lust is not only the source of sexual
sin, but sin itself. He closed the door to the pharisaical
notion that a man could undress a woman in his mind and
remain pure.

Lust is fed by whatever we've deposited in our brains
that it can get its claws on. What's in our brains is what
we've allowed in through our senses. The images and words
in our minds must come either from specific things our
eyes have seen and our ears have heard or an imaginative
conglomerate of such input.

What kind of person we are becoming is determined
by what we are taking into our brains. When we read
Scripture and good books, participate in Christ-centered
discussion, or care for the needy, we are inclining ourselves
toward righteousness.

The old saying is still true: "Sow a thought, reap an
action; sow an action, reap a habit; sow a habit, reap a character; sow a character, reap a destiny."

Actions, habits, character, and destiny all start with a
thought, and thoughts are fostered by what we choose to
take into our minds. That's why your most important sex
organ is your brain.

Are you feeding lust…or starving it?

Are you feeding your passion for Christ…or starving it?

Which desires will prove stronger? The ones you feed the most.

SETTING BOUNDARIES

To protect our purity, we need to set mental boundaries.

On a scale of one to ten, adultery or pornography addiction might be a ten, at the top of a ladder. But the question is, what were the bottom rungs of that ladder—the ones, twos, and threes? When we identify those, disaster prevention can take place.

Often we say we want purity, but then we make choices that sabotage purity. Choices have consequences. If we want different consequences we must make different choices. One man wrote to me,

> As someone who self-destructed, I'm quick to warn people of "gateway" behaviors that often lead to sins with much greater consequences. Occasional masturbation may not seem to warrant radical choices, but where will your sin lead? Will you end up with a friend's wife? With a prostitute? Maybe, if unchecked, ten years from now you'll be guilty of child sexual abuse, with news trucks pulling onto your front lawn. Sin always escalates.

How many times have I heard men say, "I'm not that bad"? I always add, "…yet."

For years I didn't go in a particular doorway to our local supermarket because of a magazine rack. Later, my mental discipline became strong enough that I could keep my eyes away. But until then I honored my boundary. It was inconvenient, but a small price to pay to guard my purity.

We have a television, but we don't have cable. Not because we believe it's wrong, but because we don't want more temptation in our home.

I'm not telling you what you have to do. Boundaries will vary from person to person. A boundary may be not standing in a checkout line where certain magazines are displayed. Or not driving in a certain part of town. Or never going on a business trip alone.

Boundaries keep temptation from getting a foothold. They are based on the premise that *our sexual purity cannot be strengthened if we keep doing what we've always done!* We must change our habits. We are sentries charged with protecting something immensely strategic. Our Commander says:

> Above all else, guard your heart [mind, inner being], for it is the wellspring of life.
>
> PROVERBS 4:23

"Above all else" means it should be at the top of our daily duty sheet. It is critical that we protect our inmost

being from new sources of temptation. We must not provide ammunition for our enemy to use against us.

Of course, your flesh will demand that you give it new
fuel. "Feed me," it will cry. But you refuse, praying this: "Turn
my eyes away from worthless things; preserve my life according to your word" (Psalm 119:37). You become part of the
answer to your prayer by turning your eyes away. (Consider
writing out this verse and posting it on your television.)

We are not to be conformed to the world, but trans-
formed by *renewing our minds* (see Romans 12:2). We're to
deny lust and put it to death when it tries to get a grip on
us (see Colossians 3:5). We're to affirm that we are new cre-
ations in Christ, covered with His righteousness (see
2 Corinthians 5:17, 21).

Your sanctified mind, fed on God's Word, nourished
by His Spirit, polices your thought life. It says yes to what
pleases Christ and no to what doesn't.

FILLING YOUR MIND WITH PURE THOUGHTS

Just for a moment, I'd like you to follow my instruction.
Ready? Okay…don't think about snakes. Don't—I repeat,
do not—think about big, slimy snakes, coming up from
your bathtub drain at night and slithering into your bed.

You heard me. *Don't think about snakes.*

Have I kept you from thinking about snakes? No. I've

encouraged you to think about them.

Now, I want you to envision your favorite dessert. Perhaps it's your mother's Dutch apple pie, or chocolate chip cookies, or Jamoca Almond Fudge ice cream, or a Butterfinger Blizzard. Just think about that mouth-watering treat.

What happened in the last few moments? You'd forgotten all about those slithering snakes…until I mentioned them again.

Our minds are not vacuums. They will be filled with *something*. Impure thoughts are pushed out by pure thoughts:

> Whatever is true, whatever is noble, whatever is right, whatever is pure…think about such things.
> PHILIPPIANS 4:8

It's difficult to delete bad files in our brain's hard drive, but we can restrict the number of *new* bad files. Then we can open many good files. This is cause and effect. The more we fill our minds with purity and the less with impurity, the greater our purity and resistance to temptation.

"We take captive every thought to make it obedient to Christ" (2 Corinthians 10:5). When the wrong thoughts come, we correct them, replacing them with God's truth.

Martin Luther said, "You can't keep the birds from flying over your head, but you can keep them from making a nest in your hair." No, we can't keep the world from throwing images at us. But we can keep them from homesteading in our minds. We can quickly evict them.

Masturbation is fueled by a roving eye and an undisciplined mind. When we turn to it, we are medicating a pain—maybe loneliness, discouragement, rejection, or fear. There is something deeper than just the obvious desire. We need to address the root issue, to ask God to meet the needs that make us vulnerable to the temptation. Self-talk helps: "Looking at this magazine really won't solve any of my problems; it will *create* problems, hurts, and loneliness."

We must do more than say, "I will not masturbate." Good intentions don't abolish lust. Unless we guard our eyes and minds, we'll fall back to old habits.

Victory is definitely possible—I spoke today with a former sex addict who hasn't masturbated for two years. But victory can't happen if we allow our minds to consume what fuels the lust that prompts the action. The key to this brother's victory is that he has guarded his mind.

While other urges exist for our physical maintenance, sex does not (see 1 Corinthians 6:12–13). We will die without food and water. We will not die without sex. No matter how strong the desire, sex is never an emergency, never a necessity. A friend told me, "No body has ever exploded due to toxic sperm buildup."

As we learn to stop feeding lust, we begin to master it. In time its demands become less pressing, more manageable.

WHAT LUST DOES TO US

Lust is mental promiscuity. That's why getting married doesn't solve the lust problem. A man who looks at other women will still do it. A man who masturbates will still do it.

A lustful person keeps moving from picture to picture, from partner to partner. Men married to beautiful women have just as high a likelihood of pornography addiction. It's a sickness of the soul. It only gets worse unless there's repentance and change. (I add *change* because many "repent" again and again, yet go right back to the bondage.)

The lustful man walks with a noose around his neck. He's an adulterer just waiting for an adulteress to come along. She may be a fantasy or a reality, but she'll show up.

Some rationalize their lust because their spouse doesn't meet their sexual needs. Where do they get their ideas of what they need? From the media, where superstud men and surgically enhanced women on starvation diets throw themselves at each other. God prescribes different qualities to look for (see 1 Peter 3:3–4).

A COVENANT WITH YOUR EYES

Job says, "I made a covenant with my eyes not to look lustfully at a girl" (Job 31:1). Job made a covenant between himself and God to guard his heart by guarding his eyes. The verses that follow spell out the terrible consequences should he not live by this covenant (see Job 31:2–12).

Have you made a contract with your eyes, not to look where they shouldn't? To immediately turn from whatever draws them to lust?

Are you practicing this purity covenant when you walk across campus? When you work out? When you drive? When you select television shows? When you're at church?

Have you announced your covenant? Have you asked others to pray for you and hold you accountable?

CLEARING OUT LUST'S POISON

Arsenic has a cumulative effect. It kills you, but not all at once. Large quantities aren't necessary. A little here, a little there, and finally...you're dead.

Sexual immorality is a killer of Christian lives and marriages. We poison ourselves daily, a little at a time. This novel, that TV show, this movie, that magazine, this calendar, that glance, this flirtatious comment, that quiet assent to a dirty story.

This arsenic of the soul poisons us gradually, so we don't feel much different than yesterday, but we've become very different than we were five years ago.

Do you believe this? If you do, say to God, "I know these sexual images are poisoning me. Give me the wisdom and resolve to turn away from them. Turn me instead to what pleases You."

In time, by eating and drinking the right things, you

can flush arsenic out of your system. But you can't recover if you don't keep *new* arsenic out!

If you really believe something is poison, and abstain from it long enough, something wonderful happens. Your desire for it *decreases*. You become healthy again. Romans 7 is painfully clear about the hold wrong desires can have on us. But many have found victory after long, weary years of lust and pornography addiction.

For decades I've believed that erotic images on television and in movies are poison. Yes, I still have a desire to look at them, but that desire is overwhelmed by an instinct to turn away. Call it whatever you wish, but turning away has become a deeply ingrained habit. Sometimes I still fail, but not nearly like I did years ago. We are creatures of habit—God's Spirit can empower us to form new habits.

By choosing to turn away from sexual temptation, by making a covenant with my eyes—and by God's enabling grace—I choose the path of life and the blessings that come with it. When I say no to temptation, I say yes to God. He is pleased and glorified.

And no one benefits more than I do.

Chapter 6

WISE STRATEGIES

Imagine someone whose weakness is eating doughnuts. His doctor says, "No more doughnuts." He vows to God, "No more doughnuts." He promises his family, "No more doughnuts." He calls the church and gets on the prayer chain. He even goes to a doughnut deliverance ministry to have the demon of doughnut desire cast out of him.

Here's a guy who means business, right?

But then what does he do? Well, if he's like a lot of us, he goes right on reading about doughnuts, listening to doughnut music, and watching television programs about making doughnuts. He spends his time with other doughnut lovers talking about doughnuts, and he jokes about doughnuts at the office, where he often glances at the doughnut calendars on the wall. He looks through the newspaper for doughnut coupons and subscribes to

Doughnut Desires, with its glossy color photos.

It's not long before he's driving the long way to work that "just happens" to go by a doughnut shop. He rolls down the window and inhales. Pretty soon he's buying the morning paper from the rack right outside the doughnut shop. He's lingering just long enough to check out doughnuts through the window.

Then he remembers he has to make a phone call, and hey, what do you know, the doughnut shop has a pay phone. And since he's there anyway, why not have a cup of coffee?

Now, remember, this man has no intention of breaking his vow and eating doughnuts. But the totally predictable and inevitable result is—what? *That he will give in and eat doughnuts!*

And can't you just hear his sad lament? *"What went wrong? I prayed! I asked others to pray. I asked God for deliverance. Why try? I give up. You do your best, and look what happens!"*

THE FIRST AND MOST BASIC STRATEGY

If we learn nothing else from the parable of the doughnuts, we should learn that sincere intentions, and even prayers, are not enough. *To have victory over temptation, we must have clear goals and sound strategies, and we must diligently carry them out.*

What's our first line of defense against impurity?

Flee from sexual immorality.
1 CORINTHIANS 6:18

When it comes to sexual temptation, it pays to be a coward. He who hesitates (and rationalizes) is lost. He who runs, lives.

Scripture puts it emphatically:

Do not set foot on the path of the wicked or walk in the way of evil men. Avoid it, do not travel on it; turn from it and go on your way.
PROVERBS 4:14–15

Joseph demonstrated this with Potiphar's wife:

And though she spoke to Joseph day after day, he refused to go to bed with her or even be with her.… She caught him by his cloak and said, "Come to bed with me!" But he left his cloak in her hand and ran out of the house.
GENESIS 39:10, 12

Joseph not only refused to go to bed with her, but refused to "even be with her." When she finally pushed herself on him he didn't stay. He ran.

Don't stay and try to "resist" temptation when you can run from it. If you're on a diet, stay away from doughnuts!

KEEP YOUR DISTANCE

If you told your children, "Don't play on the freeway," what would you expect of them? To go down by the freeway, sidle up to the edge, climb on the guardrail, dangle their legs out, or dance along the white line on the shoulder?

Obviously not. That's flirting with disaster.

"But we didn't go *on* the freeway," they might say. Maybe not. But if you keep seeing how close you can get to the freeway, it's only a matter of time until you get run over.

That's why I don't like the classic question of "How far can we go?" What are we really asking here? *How close can we get without actually sinning? Tell me where the line is so I can inch my toes right up to the edge.*

Scripture says something different: "Flee the evil desires of youth, and pursue righteousness, faith, love and peace, along with those who call on the Lord out of a pure heart" (2 Timothy 2:22).

When you're fleeing, you don't keep turning around and asking, "Is this far enough?" The spirit of obedience says, "If my Father tells me this is wrong, I'll stay away from it. And if that's the line, I'll stay twenty feet away, not two inches."

ANTICIPATE AND PREVENT TEMPTATIONS

Those whose jobs involve travel get lots of sexual temptation. Home, family, and community provide natural restraints that are left behind. Anonymity, loneliness, and leisure time often spell catastrophe.

I know godly men and women who travel frequently yet consistently have moral victory. But many others have long track records of failure. They need to stop traveling, even if it means finding another job that pays less.

At a men's conference I once asked those who travel to stand and share what they'd found helpful in resisting sexual temptation. One man told us that for years he'd watched immoral movies in hotel rooms. After repeated failures he finally decided to do something.

"Whenever I check into a hotel, I ask them to remove the television from my room. Invariably they look at me like I'm crazy. 'But sir, you don't have to turn it on.' Since I'm a paying customer, I politely insist, and I've never once been refused. Immorality is no longer just a button push away. This is how I've said 'I'm serious about this, Lord.' I've done this for a year, and it's my key to victory. Everything's changed."

This man discovered a great principle: It's always easier to *avoid* temptation than to *resist* it.

In moments of strength, make decisions that will prevent temptation in moments of weakness.

CULTIVATE YOUR INNER LIFE

There's a danger that a book like this can appear to be behavior modification. I'm well aware that simple guidelines and the "just try harder" exhortation aren't enough to break the grip of lust or the power of deeply ingrained habits. There is no "easy little formula."

I cannot emphasize enough the importance of drawing on the indwelling power of the risen Christ. Self-reformation is not enough. It may bring limited benefits but lead to self-righteousness. The Christian life is more than sin management. It's divine transformation and enablement to live righteously.

Yet Scripture commands us to do and *not* to do certain things that *are* within our power. And often, in doing these things, our hearts change. So we should take wise steps, knowing that they are not sufficient, but they are necessary. Ultimately, the battle for purity is won or lost in quietness, on our knees with God and in collaboration with our fellow soldiers.

Busyness wears down our ability to hear the promptings of God's Spirit, His Word, and His people. Fatigue makes us oblivious to what's really happening. Healthy self-examination reveals to us our "triggers"—the situations that tempt us. We then take these to God.

Time with God is the fountain from which holiness flows…and joy, and delight. It reminds us who we are…and *whose* we are. Our citizenship is in heaven (Philippians 3:20). We are "aliens and strangers on earth," who are "longing for a better country—a heavenly one" (Hebrews 11:13–16). We are here on a short-term visa. When we daily set our minds on heaven, where Christ is, He empowers us to put to death the works of the old nature—including sexual immorality, impurity, and lust (see Colossians 3:1–5).

MEMORIZE AND QUOTE SCRIPTURE

Jesus quoted Scripture to answer Satan's temptations (see Matthew 4:2–11).

When the attacks on your purity come, be ready to take up the sword of the Spirit, which is the Word of God (see Ephesians 6:17). This requires you to memorize Scripture:

> I have hidden your word in my heart that I might not sin against you.
>
> PSALM 119:11

The Purity Principle contains many Scripture passages. Pick out several that really speak to you. Write them out, carry them with you, post them prominently. When you're tempted, *talk back to the devil.* The Bible gives you the words to say. Have them ready.

PRAY AND DON'T GIVE UP

Jesus taught His disciples to *"always pray and not give up"* (Luke 18:1).

We are often brought to our knees after losing a battle. But we need to fall to our knees *before* the battle begins.

Too often we declare a truce with sin. We tolerate unrighteousness and let it claim more territory in our lives and in our homes.

Jesus says, "Don't give up! Pray for God's help." Some readers will be suspicious of this because they've heard "Just read the Bible and pray, and that will solve everything." No, it won't solve everything, but nothing will be solved without it. Jesus knew what He was talking about. So did James.

"Resist the devil, and he will flee from you" (James 4:7).

Would God tell you to abstain from impurity if that were impossible?

Many men have been defeated so long they think victory is impossible. They've given up. That guarantees they'll go right on losing. But God calls us and *empowers* us to be overcomers (see Revelation 3:5)—those who experience victory over sin.

An overcoming friend told me, *"People never change until it hurts them less to change than to stay the same."* Many Christian men—most of whom had to become desperate first—are in sexual-addiction recovery groups that have been great instruments of change in their lives. Tens of thousands of people are living proof that victory over sexual temptation is possible. And frankly, we need to hear their stories in our churches, to glorify God and bring this message of hope.

Likewise, many non-Christian men have achieved significant freedom through the secular program Sexaholics Anonymous, which uses the twelve steps of Alcoholics Anonymous. If men without Christ have made such radical changes (by affirming many biblical principles, certainly), *how dare we imagine that the Spirit of God cannot do far more in believers He indwells and empowers?*

If someone put a gun to your head and said he would pull the trigger if you looked at pornography, would you do it? No? Then you don't *have* to. You just keep putting yourself and your eyes in the wrong place. This is where you must learn to correct your wrong thinking with God's truth, saying no to your impulses and cultivating new ones.

You can turn it off, walk out, shut your eyes. You don't have to click on that link. You don't have to fondle that person or allow him or her to fondle you. There's an alternative. Draw upon your supernatural resources (see 2 Peter 1:3–4).

> For the grace of God that brings salvation…teaches us to say "No" to ungodliness and worldly passions, and to live self-controlled, upright and godly lives in this present age.
>
> TITUS 2:11–12

This is all about the great themes of Scripture: redemption and grace. Our sexual struggles should remind us of our need for grace and empowerment—and make us long for our ultimate redemption (see Romans 7:7–25).

If a lifetime of purity seems inconceivable to you, commit yourself in twenty-four-hour increments. Do you want freedom from the actions and obsessions of lust? Get help. Be wise. Avoid temptation. Go to Christ. Experience His sufficiency. Draw on His power.

And when the first twenty-four hours are over, and you've tasted of the Lord and seen He is good (see Psalm 34:8), commit to the next twenty-four hours. Depend on Him one day at a time.

Never underestimate Christ. Sin is not more powerful than God. Don't imagine there can't be victory until we get to heaven. God says otherwise. We're not to wait for victory. We're to live in it (see 1 John 5:4).

Chapter 7

GETTING RADICAL

Suppose I said, "There's a great-looking girl down the street. Let's go look through her window and watch her undress, then pose for us naked, from the waist up. Then this girl and her boyfriend will get in a car and have sex—let's listen and watch the windows steam up!"

You'd be shocked. You'd think, *What a pervert!*

But suppose instead I said, "Hey, come on over. Let's watch *Titanic."*

Christians recommend this movie, church youth groups view it together, and many have shown it in their homes. Yet the movie contains *precisely* the scenes I described.

So, as our young men lust after the girl on the screen, our young women are trained in how to get a man's attention.

How does something shocking and shameful somehow

become acceptable because we watch it through a television instead of a window?

In terms of the lasting effects on our minds and morals, *what's the difference?*

Yet many think, *Titanic? Wonderful! It wasn't even rated R!*

Every day Christians across the country, including many church leaders, watch people undress through the window of television. We peek on people committing fornication and adultery, which our God calls an abomination.

We've become voyeurs, Peeping Toms, entertained by sin.

NORMALIZING EVIL

The enemy's strategy is to normalize evil. Consider young people struggling with homosexual temptation. How does it affect them when they watch popular television dramas where homosexual partners live together in apparent normality?

Parents who wouldn't dream of letting a dirty-minded adult baby-sit their children do it every time they let their kids surf the channels.

Not only we, but our children become desensitized to immorality. Why are we surprised when our son gets a girl pregnant if we've allowed him to watch hundreds of immoral acts and hear thousands of sexual innuendos?

"But it's just one little sex scene."

Suppose I offered you a cookie, saying, "A few mouse

droppings fell in the batter, but for the most part it's a great cookie—you won't even notice."

"To fear the LORD is to hate evil" (Proverbs 8:13). When we're being entertained by evil, how can we hate it? *How can we be pure when we amuse ourselves with impurity?*

God warns us not to talk about sex inappropriately:

> But among you there must not be even a hint of sexual immorality, or of any kind of impurity…because these are improper for God's holy people. Nor should there be obscenity, foolish talk or coarse joking, which are out of place.
>
> EPHESIANS 5:3–4

How do our favorite dramas and sitcoms stand up to these verses? How about *Seinfeld* and other nightly reruns? Do they contain "even a hint of sexual immorality" or "coarse joking"? If we can listen to late night comedians' monologues riddled with immoral references, are we really fearing God and hating evil?

JESUS, THE RADICAL

Consider Christ's words:

> "You have heard that it was said, 'Do not commit adultery.' But I tell you that anyone who looks at a woman lustfully has already committed adultery

with her in his heart. If your right eye causes you
to sin, gouge it out and throw it away. It is better
for you to lose one part of your body than for your
whole body to be thrown into hell. And if your
right hand causes you to sin, cut it off and throw
it away. It is better for you to lose one part of your
body than for your whole body to go into hell."

MATTHEW 5:27–30

Why does Jesus paint this shocking picture? I believe
He wants us to take radical steps, to do *whatever is necessary*
to deal with sexual temptation.

Now, the hand and eye are *not* the causes of sin. A
blind man can still lust and a man without a hand can still
steal. But the eye is a means of access for both godly and
ungodly input. And the hand is a means of performing
righteous or sinful acts. We must therefore govern what the
eye looks at and the hand does.

If we take Jesus seriously, we need to think far more
radically about sexual purity.

DOING WHAT IT TAKES

The battle is too intense, and the stakes are too high to
approach purity casually or gradually.

So...if you can't keep your eyes away from those
explicit images, don't ever go to a video rental store.

Come on. Everybody goes into those stores.

No. If it causes you to sin, you shouldn't. Period.

Do your thoughts trip you up when you're with a certain person? Stop hanging out with them. Does a certain kind of music charge you up erotically? Stop listening to it. Do you make phone calls you shouldn't? Block 900 phone sex numbers so you can't call them from your home.

If these things seem like crutches, fine. Use whatever crutches you need to help you walk.

Some men fall into mental adultery through lingerie ads, billboards, women joggers in tight pants, women with low cut blouses or short skirts, cheerleaders or dancers, movies, TV shows, and commercials of the beer-and-bikini variety. Some men's weakness is the Sunday newspaper's ad inserts or nearly *any* magazine.

So, STOP LOOKING. And then STOP PUTTING YOURSELF IN THE POSITION TO LOOK!

If you have to get rid of your TV to guard your purity, do it.

If it means you can't go to games because of how dancers or cheerleaders dress and perform, so be it. If it means you have to lower your head and close your eyes, so be it. If you're embarrassed to do that, stay home.

Tell your wife about your struggles. Or if you're single, tell a godly friend. If you need to drop the newspaper because of those ads, fine. If you need your wife to go through it first and pull out the offending inserts, ask her.

Years ago I started tearing off and trashing suggestive covers of *TV Guide*. My wife picked up on this, and now she usually does it before I see it. I'm grateful for her help. (Of course, some magazines shouldn't be in the home in the first place—including Victoria's Secret catalogues.)

Romans 13:14 instructs us to "make no provision for the flesh" (NASB). *It's a sin to deliberately put ourselves in a position where we'll likely commit sin.* Whether it's the lingerie department, the swimming pool, or the workout room at an athletic club, if it trips you up, *stay away from it.*

Proverbs describes the loose woman meeting up with the foolish man after dark (see Proverbs 7:8–9). We must stay away from people, places, and contexts that make sin more likely.

If it's certain bookstores, hangouts, or old friends from high school, STAY AWAY FROM THEM. If cable or satellite TV or network TV, the Internet, or computers are your problem, GET RID OF THEM.

Just say NO to whatever is pulling you away from Jesus. *Remember, if you want a different outcome, you must make different choices.*

If you can't be around women wearing swimsuits without looking and lusting, then don't go on vacation where women wear swimsuits. If that means not going water-skiing or to a favorite resort, fine. If it means being unable to go on a church-sponsored retreat, don't go.

Sound drastic? Compare it to gouging out an eye or cutting off a hand!

When our family was going on a vacation in the sun, I e-mailed my sons-in-law and said, "Let's not do this unless we can agree together to turn our eyes away from the women and their swimsuits. If we can't do that, we shouldn't go." They're godly young men and they fully agreed, as I knew they would. We became each other's allies in purity.

For many men, the battle gets tougher after dark. Web porn and phone sex lines flourish late at night. The solution may be a hard and fast rule. Don't stay up later than your wife, or no television or Internet after your wife's in bed.

If you're falling, get rid of what's tripping you up.

"BUT…"

"But there are hardly any decent TV shows anymore." Then stop watching TV. Read books. Have conversations.

"But all the newer novels have sex scenes." Then read the old novels. Read fiction from Christian publishers.

"But I've subscribed to Sports Illustrated *for years, back before they had the swimsuit issue."* They have it now. So drop your subscription. And tell them why.

"But it's almost impossible to rent a movie without sex and offensive language." There are Christian movie-review sites that can help you make good selections for family viewing.[3] There are also services which offer edited movies,

television adaptors which edit profanity, and DVD software that cuts offensive scenes from movies.

But suppose there were no decent movies—what then? I enjoy good movies, but the Bible never commands us "Watch movies." It does command us "Guard your heart."

It's a battle—battles get bloody. *Do whatever it takes* to walk in purity!

A friend wrote a daily contract that asks these questions: "Are you willing to do whatever's necessary to protect your sexual sobriety? Ask God for help? Call on others? Go to meetings? Read literature? Set boundaries and not cross them? Be brutally honest?"

Too Radical?

"But you're talking about withdrawing from the culture. What you're saying is too radical."

No, what *I'm* saying is nothing. *Jesus* said, "If it would keep you from sexual temptation, you'd be better off poking out your eye and cutting off your hand." Now *that's* radical.

I've prayed, "Lord, before I would ever betray my wife and commit adultery, please kill me." I heard Bill Bright pray that years ago, and I know he was serious. So am I.

Many claim they're serious about purity, but then they say, "No way; I'm not going to give up cable TV," or "I'm not going to have my wife hold the computer password."

Followers of Jesus have endured torture and given their

lives in obedience to Him. And we're whining about giving up *cable?*

When Jesus called us to take up our crosses and follow Him (see Matthew 10:38), didn't that imply sacrifices greater than forgoing Internet access?

How sold out are you to the battle for purity? How desperate are you to have victory over sin? How radical are you willing to get for your Lord? How much do you want the joy and peace that can be found only in Him?

Purity comes only to those who truly want it.

CONTROLLING THE INTERNET

Use family-friendly Internet service providers.[4] Install a pornography-filtering program on your computer, realizing it can't screen out everything. Ask someone else to hold the password. Ask someone to regularly check your internet usage history to confirm you're not compromising your walk with God.

Move computers to high-traffic areas. Unless you have a proven history of going on-line safely, don't log on to the Internet if you're alone. Be sure the monitor always faces an open door, where others can see what you're looking at (see 1 Corinthians 10:13). Check out practical resources for Internet accountability.[5]

If you're still losing the battle, disconnect from the Internet. If that's not enough, get rid of the computer.

TAKING CHARGE OF THE TV

Consult a schedule to choose appropriate programs. Channel-surfing invites temptation.

Keep your television unplugged, store it in a closet, or put it in the garage to prevent mindless flip-on.

Use the "off" switch freely. Use the remote quickly when temptation comes. Have a safe channel ready to turn to.

Don't allow young children to choose their own programs. As they get older they can choose, but parents have veto power. Avoid multiple televisions that split the family and leave children unsupervised. Don't use television as a baby-sitter.

Spend an hour reading Scripture, a Christian book, or participating in a ministry for each hour you watch TV. Even when television isn't bad, it often keeps us from what's better.

Drop cable, HBO, your satellite dish, or your TV if it is promoting ungodliness in your home. (This isn't legalism—it's discipleship.)

Periodically "fast" from television for a week or a month. Watch what happens; see if you like what you can do with all that time (including feeding your passion for Christ).

Chapter 8

GUIDELINES
FOR SINGLES

A large percentage of the population is single. This includes young people, but also adults who've never married, and those who become single through death or divorce.

For the young, the unprecedented combination of leisure time, money, and transportation is historically unique. Add to this the lack of parental supervision and the large gap between the average age of puberty and marriage. Mix in the media's saturation with sex and its portrayal of premarital sex as normal. The result is overwhelming temptation to single people, both younger and older.

Clearly, if they are to live righteously, single Christians must use wise strategies.

Scripture warns against man-made rules involving a

"harsh treatment of the body," but lacking "value in restraining sensual indulgence" (Colossians 2:20–23).

The guidelines I'm proposing are valuable if and only if they are biblical and wise. But guidelines are not inherently legalistic. The book of Proverbs calls us to live wisely, exercising God-honoring common sense.

We are told to be like soldiers, athletes, and farmers (2 Timothy 2:3–6). Each is a disciplined adherent to proven standards. God calls us to exercise self-control, a fruit of the Spirit (Galatians 5:22–23).

How Far Should Singles Go?

God made sex drives. When those drives are stimulated, they move toward a climax. This is a simple fact of biology. Caressing each other in sexually stimulating ways is foreplay. And foreplay is designed by God to culminate in sexual intercourse.

Logically, then, since intercourse is forbidden outside marriage, so is foreplay. Since sexual intercourse before marriage is wrong, it is also wrong to engage in activity that propels mind and body toward it.

This means that the line must be drawn before either person becomes sexually stimulated. Fondling—and anything else that results in a turn-on—is forbidden.

Once you let your body cross the line, it will neither

know nor care about your Christian convictions. Men are more quickly and easily stimulated than women. A woman often thinks extended kisses and hugs are fine, but the man is sexually stimulated and is tempted to push for more. You must make sure you draw the line far enough back that *neither* of you crosses it.

If one of you begins to be stimulated even by apparently innocent physical contact, then both of you should back off immediately. If you don't, you're choosing to stay in a canoe headed toward a waterfall. Those who engage in sexual stimulation should not be surprised when they finally have intercourse. It's simply the natural, predictable result of the choices they've made.

If you want a different outcome, make different choices.

CHOOSE FRIENDS WISELY

Do not be misled: "Bad company corrupts good character."

1 CORINTHIANS 15:33

It's our nature to be influenced by our surroundings. When we put ourselves in a godly atmosphere with godly people, we are influenced toward godliness. When we put ourselves in an ungodly atmosphere with ungodly people, we are influenced toward ungodliness.

He who walks with the wise grows wise, but a companion of fools suffers harm.

PROVERBS 13:20

We become like the people we spend time with. God speaks of "lovers of pleasure rather than lovers of God" and warns us, "Have nothing to do with them" (2 Timothy 3:4–5).

DATING IS AN OPTION...NOT A NECESSITY

Much sexual temptation is generated by our social custom of coupling and isolating young people. This stands in stark contrast to the Hebrew culture, and others, which require that young single people spend time together only when adults are present.

You can enjoy fun, positive friendships with people of the opposite sex and be involved in all sorts of activities without coupling up with one person. If you're interested in the case for courtship rather than dating, see *I Kissed Dating Goodbye* by Joshua Harris.

The following guidelines are excerpted from a sixteen-page handout on purity I wrote for my daughters and the young men desiring to spend time with them.[6] My wife and I went through it with both, point by point each time. If you do choose to date, these guidelines may be helpful:

- If you're a Christian, date only Christians (see 2 Corinthians 6:14).
- If you're a committed disciple, date only committed disciples.
- Christ is with you all evening—wherever you go and whatever you do.
- Remember your date is your brother or sister, not your "lover" (see 1 Timothy 5:1–2).
- Go out in groups, not alone.
- Focus on talk, not touch; conversation, not contact.
- Avoid fast-moving relationships or instant intimacy.
- Plan the entire evening in advance, with no gaps.
- Avoid setups—never be alone: on a couch, in a car late at night, in a house or bedroom.
- Be accountable to someone about your purity.
- Imagine your parents and church leaders are watching you through the window. God *is* watching (see Jeremiah 16:17).
- Write out your own standards and enforce them yourself—never depend on someone else.
- Don't do anything with your date you wouldn't want someone else doing with your future mate.
- Beware of the "moral wear down" of long dating relationships and long engagements. Once young people and parents agree on marriage, it's dangerous to wait longer than necessary (see 1 Corinthians 7: 8–9).

Chapter 9

GUIDELINES
FOR COUPLES
AND PARENTS

Countless marriages have been destroyed when casual relationships at work, school, and even at church turned into infatuation.

When you talk with people, talk about your spouse and your kids. Be careful what you think, and what you say with your eyes or body language. Even if you're not struggling with attraction to them, you don't know what they're thinking.

Tell yourself, "This could become an attraction that could threaten all I hold dear. I will not let that happen." You don't need to be paranoid—you *do* need to be alert.

Cut through Satan's smoke screen before the smoke's so thick you choke on it. Run from the lie before it gets its claws around your throat.

We must develop an early detection system to spot moral danger before we're sinking in quicksand. *A relationship can be inappropriate long before it becomes sexual.*

CULTIVATE AND GUARD YOUR MARRIAGE

Every adultery begins with deception, and most deception begins with seemingly innocent secrets ("He doesn't need to know this"). If you're married, regularly evaluate your relationship with your mate. Watch for the red flags of discontentment and a diminishing sexual relationship. Talk openly. Work it through, even if it's painful.

Be sensitive to your spouse's sexual needs. Remember that marriage involves a sexual responsibility—"do not deprive each other" (1 Corinthians 7:5). Communicate honestly about this. Don't harbor resentment. If one of you feels you need sex more (or less) often, set some specific times so that neither of you have to wonder when it's the right time. (Spontaneity isn't everything!)

Date your spouse—put it in your schedule. At work, surround yourself with reminders of your spouse and children. When away, call frequently.

Be fiercely loyal to your spouse; speak highly of them. Don't share marriage problems with someone of the opposite sex, unless it's in a familial or professional relationship. Even then, be careful.

Pray with and for each other. Take care of your physical health; be as attractive to your mate as you can. Be modest with others in public, and sexy with your spouse in private—never the opposite!

Work hard to bring your spouse into your world. Talk about your jobs. Talk about your struggles, disappointments, and concerns. *Listen to one another.* (Put down that newspaper.) Don't live two separate lives under one roof. This is the first step toward an affair with "someone who understands me and my world."

Christian marriages face the same heartaches, struggles, and frustrations as other marriages. (But we have supernatural resources to deal with them.) Our marriages can become plagued with resentment, boredom, or hurt. This makes us vulnerable to Satan's lie about the intrigue and excitement of a new person. The answer is not a new person, but a fresh appreciation of the "old" person.

REKINDLE ATTRACTION TO YOUR MATE

A friend shared that he was no longer attracted to his wife. He committed himself to praying daily that God would make her the most attractive woman in the world to him. Within a month that prayer was decisively answered. She didn't change. He did. After hearing his story, another man did the same and also saw dramatic results. Both of their marriages have been revitalized.

Train your eyes to turn away from stimulating images and fix them upon your spouse. *When your sex drive is activated, lock it on your partner.* Appetites can be cultivated. What we focus on shapes our desires. By denying errant appetites and meditating on the right things—including being "captivated" by your wife's love (Proverbs 5:19)—you can train yourself to desire what's proper.

Treasure your marriage partner. Recognize that his or her qualities aren't the result of airbrushing, camera angles, and cosmetic surgery. They won't fade as those do, but will endure and deepen. Limit your eyes to your mate, and he or she will become the true desire of your heart.

Sometimes our marriage problems need assistance from the outside. Get help *now*.

Avail yourself of Christian books and other resources geared to marital enrichment. FamilyLife ministries offers wonderful weekend conferences that can be a great asset in strengthening marriages.[7]

BE HONEST WITH YOUR MATE

A woman told me that a year earlier her husband came to her in tears, confessing his attraction to a coworker. He was under constant temptation and felt himself slipping. He committed himself to back off from the relationship and asked his wife to understand and pray for him. She was hurt but realized she needed to help him rather than feel sorry for herself.

The result? Not only did he back off, but through his wife's support they drew closer together than ever. In tears she told me, "Two months ago my husband died without warning. If he hadn't been honest with me that night, he would have had an affair with that woman—and likely would have left me. He would have died unready to meet God, and I would have lived the rest of my life grieving over his affair. But that isn't what happened. His last words to me were, 'I love you,' and I know it was true—he'd proven it by his actions. I thank God every day that I think of him with complete respect and admiration for loving God and me enough to be honest about his struggles."

Lust thrives on secrecy. Nothing defuses it like exposure. (One man told me, "We're only as sick as our deepest secret.") Honest communication between husband and wife will make them allies, not adversaries. While there's initial pain in discussing sexual temptation, there's also relief and growth.

"Confess your sins to each other and pray for each other so that you may be healed" (James 5:16). While your spouse may be unaware of your sin, she has been deeply affected by it. If you don't confess it, you cheat her twice: first in the sin itself, and second by not allowing her to forgive you or respond as she chooses. (Don't feel compelled, however, to reveal every sordid detail. A simple statement of facts is sufficient.)

Husbands, ask your wife's help in the ways we've already mentioned. Wives, ask your husband about his temptations. What can you do for him? Be grateful if he's open with you. Don't be naive. Too many women are ignorant of the battles in male minds. Don't recommend that your husband and best friend jog together. If you've agreed he should use the Internet only when you're nearby, don't think, *I'm going to bed; he'll be fine.*

Don't act superior because he struggles where you don't. Have you ever succumbed to fantasies about men, to soap operas or steamy romance novels, to gossip or slander? Confess your sins to him, too. He needs you as a friend and ally, not an adversary.

RAISING PURE CHILDREN

Sometimes our children may fail to listen to us. Rarely will they fail to imitate us. Sons learn from their fathers whether to stare at—or look away from—dancers, cheerleaders, and commercials with seductive women. Daughters also notice where dad's eyes go—and mom's.

The greatest legacy we can give our children is to show them a loving, affectionate, and pure marriage.

Train children in choice and consequence, wisdom and

foolishness, as exemplified in Proverbs. Teach them to love righteousness and hate sin (see Psalm 97:10). Teach them self-control—the ability to say no in other areas will carry over to sexual purity.

Parents should exercise gracious but firm control over their children's friendships and media habits. We should avoid a double standard that says children shouldn't watch impure programs on television, but it's okay for adults.

Protect your children. Would any thinking parents pile a stack of pornographic magazines in their son's bedroom closet, then tell him, "We trust you not to look at them"? This is what we do when we allow him a computer with Internet access in his bedroom.

Parents need to screen their children's clothing. Men are responsible to help their wives and daughters understand why this is so important. Women, please believe us—when we say a prom dress, shorts, top or swimsuit is inappropriate, we know *exactly* what we're talking about.

YOUR CHILD'S SEX EDUCATION

Every child receives a sex education. The only questions are: (1) When? (2) Where? (3) From whom? Parents should be their ultimate sex educators.

If you don't know all the facts, don't be embarrassed. Find them out from appropriate sources. Speak of sex not just as biology, but in the context of values, responsibility, and marriage.

Know your child—what he's ready for and what he isn't. Answer all questions honestly, in an age-appropriate way. Tell your kids as much as they need to know now—not less, not more.

Don't procrastinate. Your child's welfare is at stake. Don't have your first talk about sex with your pregnant fifteen-year-old.

Be positive. Talk about how *good* sex can be inside marriage. Don't be ashamed to talk about what God wasn't ashamed to create.

If anyone else is teaching your children about sex, find out exactly what's being said.

Teach and model modesty in the home. Where else will your children learn it?

Chapter 10

CONFESSION, ACCOUNTABILITY, AND COUNTING THE COST

*If we confess our sins, he is faithful and just and will
forgive us our sins and purify us from all unrighteousness.*
1 JOHN 1:9

Like David, who committed adultery and murder, we must
repent thoroughly, without rationalizing (see Psalm 51).

We dare not postpone confession. "He who conceals
his sins does not prosper, but whoever confesses and
renounces them finds mercy" (Proverbs 28:13).

True repentance means removing temptation and changing the choices that unnecessarily expose us. "But I can't help the first look." Sometimes that's true. But choosing to go to a beach full of women in bikinis, then saying "I can't help the first look" is rationalizing. Going to a movie and having to look at the floor is better than watching. But it's smarter to leave...and smarter yet not to go in the first place. Repentance means not just *turning* from impurity, but *keeping* ourselves from where we'll have to turn.

If you're single and no longer a virgin, you can commit yourself to secondary virginity—to remain sexually pure from this day forward. Forgiveness doesn't mean there are no residual effects of past sin, but it means you can stop the damage today and enjoy the blessings of purity from now on.

Don't be discouraged by what I've said about the consequences of sin. It's true, but it's also true that God is sovereign and gracious; He brings beauty out of ashes. No matter what we've done, the moment we repent and embrace His forgiveness, we can be right in the center of God's will.

He is the father who, seeing his prodigal son return home, is so "filled with compassion for him; he ran to his son, threw his arms around him and kissed him" (Luke 15:20). He will demonstrate His amazing grace to us in ways that will delight us. He can cleanse us and make us holy vessels, "useful to the Master" (2 Timothy 2:21). We forfeit certain things through sin, but we do *not* forfeit God's forgiving grace.

SEEK ACCOUNTABILITY

Be an active part of your local Bible-believing Christ-centered church (see Hebrews 10:25). Surround yourself with friends who raise the moral bar, not lower it (see 1 Corinthians 15:33). Ask an older, mature Christian to mentor you as you seek to walk in purity (see Titus 2:2, 6–8).

Left alone, you cannot win the battle. Use the buddy system. Have someone you can call day or night for help and prayer. I have a friend who phones one of his accountability partners every day, regardless of whether he feels temptation. Rather than just tell each other after they've fallen, they prevent falls by staying ahead of sin.

Nearly twenty years ago, our pastoral staff meetings were large enough to let individuals blend into the woodwork a little and hide from direct accountability. As a result, I met with two other pastors weekly, then started another accountability group with four laymen. We began with Scripture we'd memorized. Then each person would answer key questions:

How are you doing with God? With your mate? Children? What temptations are you facing, and how are you dealing with them? How has your thought life been this week? Have you been spending regular time in the Word and prayer? Who have you been sharing the gospel with? Have you lied in any of your answers? How can we pray for you and help you?

Men in both groups said this was the most meaningful ninety minutes of their week. For most it was the first time a brother in Christ had *ever* asked them these questions.

Usually those who fall into sexual sin have lacked no-nonsense, bare-knuckle accountability. The more visible Christian leaders become, the more they *need* accountability—and the less they usually get it.

I need accountability, you need it, your pastor needs it, your spouse needs it, and your kids need it. Everyone does. When I'm pursuing secret sin, the last thing I want to do is be with serious Christians. The time I most need accountability is the time I'll most likely withdraw from it.

One evening I was undergoing strong sexual temptation. It wouldn't let up. Finally I called a brother I was to have breakfast with the next morning. I said, "Please pray for me, and promise to ask me tomorrow morning what I did." He agreed. The moment I put down the phone, the temptation was gone. Why? I'd like to say it was because I'm so spiritual. The truth is, there was no way I was going to face this guy the next morning and have to tell him I'd sinned.

My friend was my 911 call. How much better to get immediate help, which *prevents* sin, rather than reporting to my group next week, "I blew it." Honesty about our sin is good—but honesty about our temptation is even better.

Who are your 911 friends?

Those who've gotten help for sexual addictions know they must lean on others committed to purity. This battle isn't won alone. When an addict, in bondage to sin, admits "I am powerless to change," he can then draw upon power outside himself—God above all, but also comrades in the fight. For these men, a weekly meeting isn't enough. Daily phone calls and frequent meetings may be needed. But there's hope and help—for all willing to receive it. There are groups and ministries dedicated to aiding those who want to escape from bondage.[8]

COUNT THE COST

The consequences of premarital sex are serious and ongoing—disappointing your Lord, losing your virginity, mental images that can plague you, greater possibility of extramarital sex, unwanted pregnancy, and disease.

Premarital sex is a sin, but pregnancy isn't. Don't make your child pay the price. Others will help you, and you'll save yourself torment, if you let your child live.[9]

Years ago my friend Alan Hlavka and I each developed a list of the consequences that would result from our immorality. The lists were devastating, and they spoke to us more powerfully than any sermon. Periodically, especially when traveling, I'd reread this list, until I memorized it. It cut like a knife through fogs of rationalization. It filled me with healthy fear.

What follows is an edited version of our combined lists. You might revise this list to make it your own.

What would my adultery do?

- Drag in the mud the reputation of my Lord.
- Make me have to look into His face one day and tell Him why I did it.
- Cause untold hurt to Nanci, my loyal wife and best friend.
- Forfeit Nanci's respect and trust.
- Permanently injure my credibility with my beloved daughters, Karina and Angie.
- Bring great shame to my family.
- Inflict hurt on my church and friends, especially those I've led to Christ and discipled. (List names.)
- Bring an irretrievable loss of years of witnessing to relatives and friends.
- Bring pleasure to Satan, God's enemy.
- Possibly give me a sexually transmitted disease, posing a risk to Nanci.
- Lose my self-respect, discredit my name, and invoke lifelong embarrassment upon myself.

This is less than half of the items from the list.

If we would rehearse in advance the devastating consequences of immorality, we would be far less prone to commit it.

A BATTLE WE CAN WIN

In J. R. R. Tolkien's *The Hobbit,* no one was seemingly more invincible than Smaug, the mighty dragon. But unknown to Smaug, there was one small chink in the armor of his underbelly. That was all it took for Bard the hunter, a skilled archer.

Unaware of his weakness and underestimating his opponents, Smaug failed to protect himself. Bard's arrow pierced his heart, and the lake people were saved.

An exciting story with a happy ending. But when it's a Christian felled by the evil one, the ending is tragic. Satan knows the chinks in our armor! His aim is deadly.

As I look at myself and my brothers and sisters in Christ, I'm deeply concerned at how careless and morally soft we've become. At times we are frighteningly weak in our exercise of sexual purity. We watch and are amused by what offends a holy God. Our tolerance for impurity keeps expanding. Sin sneaks in under our radar. We make ourselves defenseless.

Men and women desensitized by immorality, or teetering on the verge of affairs, sit in church calloused, or writhing in guilt and agony, feeling like the hypocrites they are and hating themselves for it. They may still attend, but they distance themselves from God and others.

Our God longs to forgive and restore us, delivering us from the road to death and setting us on the path of life.

It's time to take a close look at our minds, words, and actions. Like the Greek warrior Achilles, the strongest of us may appear unassailable to ourselves or to those who respect us. But one arrow to our heel proves otherwise.

Think honestly and carefully—is susceptibility to sexual impurity your Achilles' heel? Is it a chink in your armor? If so, following the guidelines of this book may be more than a nice precaution—it may actually save your life and family from ruin. It may keep you from forfeiting God's blessing for your future.

Those whose lives and families have been devastated should rejoice in His forgiving grace. Don't lose hope. God is not finished with you. Be patient, even though you're reaping consequences of past actions, some not your own.

Trust God that in time you will reap vast rewards for the purity and faith you exercise today—"you know that the Lord will reward everyone for whatever good he does" (Ephesians 6:8).

"ON YOUR WAY IN SAFETY"

God doesn't want us to live each day paralyzed by the fear of a sudden fall. In the context of resisting sexual temptation, the wise man says:

> My son, preserve sound judgment and discernment,
>   do not let them out of your sight;
> they will be life for you,
>   an ornament to grace your neck.
> Then you will go on your way in safety,
>   and your foot will not stumble;
> when you lie down, you will not be afraid;
>   when you lie down, your sleep will be sweet.
> Have no fear of sudden disaster
>   or of the ruin that overtakes the wicked,
> for the LORD will be your confidence
>   and will keep your foot from being snared.
>   PROVERBS 3:21–26

If we walk daily with Christ, guarding our hearts and keeping the covenant with our eyes, then—and only then—we can go our way "in safety" and "not be afraid."

A FINAL QUESTION

Are you ready to commit—or recommit—yourself to a life of sexual purity? Now's the time. Nothing's more fleeting than the moment of conviction.

God made a universe in which righteousness is always rewarded, and unrighteousness is always punished.

Purity is always smart; impurity is always stupid.

> "I the LORD search the heart and examine the mind, to reward a man according to his conduct, according to what his deeds deserve."
>
> JEREMIAH 17:10

Live in such a way as to hear your Lord say to you one day, "Well done, my good and faithful servant!"

When we hear Him say those incredible words, we will know that any sacrifice we made was nothing.

Honor God by living in sexual purity. If you do, you'll experience His blessing and rewards not only today, tomorrow, and ten years from now, but throughout eternity.

If we plant purity today, we will reap a rich harvest.

And, by the grace of God, we will look back on our lives not with regret, but with joyful gratitude.

We would love to hear your comments about this book.
Please contact the publisher at:
www.lifechangebooks.com
or the author at:
www.epm.org

Notes

1. See Randy Alcorn, *The Law of Rewards* (Wheaton, Il.: Tyndale House Publishers, 2003).

2. John Piper, *Future Grace* (Sisters, Ore.: Multnomah Publishers, Inc., 1995), 336.

3. See christiananswers.net/spotlight/movies; www.movieguide.org; or www.family.org/pplace/pi

4. See www.afafilter.com

5. See www.covenanteyes.com

6. See www.epm.org/sexpur.html, or call 1-503-663-6481 for a copy.

7. FamilyLife ministries, 1-800-FLTODAY, www.familylife.com

8. See Heart to Heart Counseling Center, 1-719-278-3708, www.sexaddict.com; Sexaholics Anonymous, 1-615-331-6230, www.sa.org; for a list of recovery groups and resources, see www.sexaddict.com/Links.html

9. If you're pregnant and need help, you can get free confidential assistance by calling Care Net at 1-800-395-HELP.

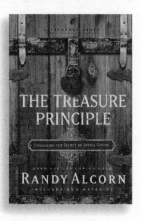
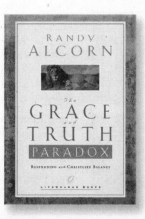

Spine-tingling fiction from...
RANDY ALCORN

Lord Foulgrin's Letters

A creative, insightful, and biblical depiction of spiritual warfare, this book will guide readers to Christ-honoring counterstrategies for putting on the full armor of God and resisting the devil. Revised, shortened version.

ISBN 1-57673-861-2
Also available in audiocassette ISBN 1-57673-715-2

The Ishbane Conspiracy

Midterms, dating, and messy dorm rooms are the least of their worries. Four college students must contend with demonic influence in a life-or-death battle for their souls.

ISBN 1-57673-817-5
Also available in audiocassette ISBN 1-57673-993-7

Deadline

After tragedy strikes those closest to him, journalist Jake Woods is drawn into a complex murder investigation that forces him to ultimately seek answers to the meaning of his existence.

ISBN 1-57673-316-5
Audio read by Frank Muller ISBN 1-57673-318-1

Dominion

When two murders drag a columnist into the world of gangs and racial conflict, he seeks revenge for the killings and answers to hard issues regarding race and faith.

ISBN 1-57673-661-X
Audio read by Frank Muller ISBN 1-57673-682-2